Letters to Anne

GWENNETH LEANE

A DEVOTIONAL

PUBLISHER
Kylie Margaret Leane
kmlpublishing.com

COVER ART/DESIGN/ILLUSTRATIONS
Kylie Leane

© 2020 Gwenneth Leane
All rights reserved.

No portion of this publication may be reproduced or transmitted,
in any form or by any means, without the prior written permission of either copyright owner or publisher of this book.

LETTERS TO ANNE:
A DEVOTIONAL
PUBLICATION HISTORY

Paperback Edition / July 2020 Gwenneth
ISBN: 978-0-9944382-7-0

PRINTED IN AUSTRALIA

A catalogue record for this book is available from the National Library of Australia

For information address:
gwen.leane@gmail.com
authorkylieleane@gmail.com

Gwenneth's Blog can be found online at:
Gwen's Goss

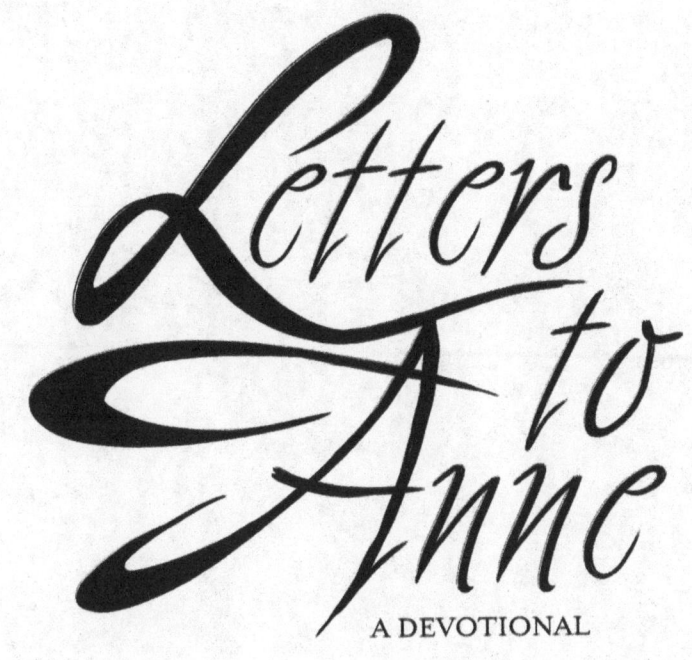

A DEVOTIONAL

GWENNETH LEANE

Decision is the key to destiny.

"God, can you be merciful and send me off to hell and lock me in forever?"

"No, Pilgrim, I will not send you there,
but if you chose to go there,
I could never lock you out."

The Singer Trilogy by Calvin Miller

GWENNETH LEANE

Thought for the Day:

'The blessing, the honour, the glory, the power belong to the one sitting on the throne, to the Lamb forever and ever.'
Revelation 5: 13 LB

Prayer:

Thank you, Father, for the Glory-man Jesus who dwells within us. Grant us a more apparent revelation of this truth.

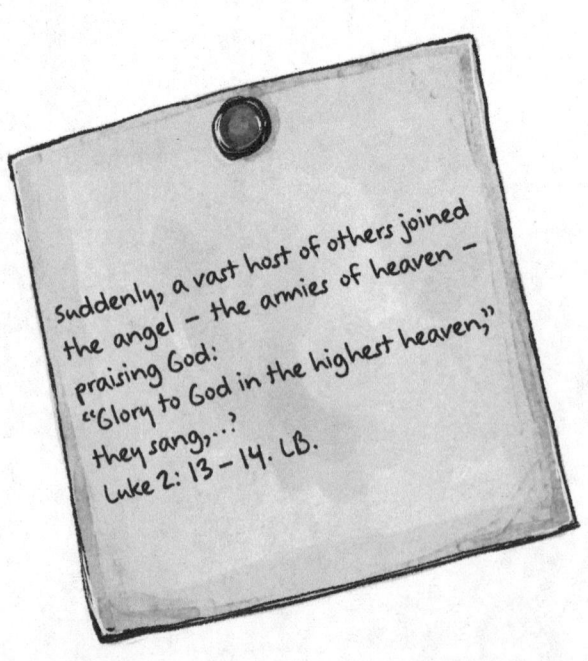

Suddenly, a vast host of others joined the angel — the armies of heaven — praising God:
"Glory to God in the highest heaven," they sang,...'
Luke 2: 13 – 14. LB.

Letters to Anne

Anne, my dear friend,

Greetings to you.

I wonder if you have ever thought about the Glory of the Lord.

I have collected some thoughts about Glory.

A scripture reading for meditation:

Psalm 24: 1 – 10. LB *'Who is this King of Glory? The Commander of all of heaven's armies!...'*

'Glory. From Glory to Glory he's changing me, changing me, changing me.' These words are a line in a old chorus. I used to sing them with great gusto. I did believe the Lord was changing me but I felt it would be realized when I reached heaven.

The line of another chorus comes to mind, *'Heaven came down, and glory shone around.'* I believed that when the angels sang at Jesus birth, heaven did come down. The skies lit up, and Glory shone around. But it was only to announce Jesus birth.

I realize now heaven did come to earth in many ways at Jesus' birth. The Glory was Jesus; he is the Glory. We don't need to wait for the Glory, or make ourselves worthy of the Glory or pray for a UFO kind of experience. When we have Jesus, we have the Glory. When we become believers of Jesus, his Glory fills us. We then are the Glory of God. We are full of the Glory-man, Jesus. We need nothing more or less.

In Christ, I am being changed from Glory to Glory because Glory – the man Jesus, came down and shone all around.

He never left, he lives in us.

GWENNETH LEANE

Thought for the Day:

You may be struggling, but keep declaring, '...the blessings fall on me. I'm prosperous. I have the favour of God.' Every time you say it, you're getting closer to seeing it come true.

Prayer:

May the Father of our Lord Jesus Christ give to us the Spirit of wisdom and revelation in the knowledge of him (Jesus).

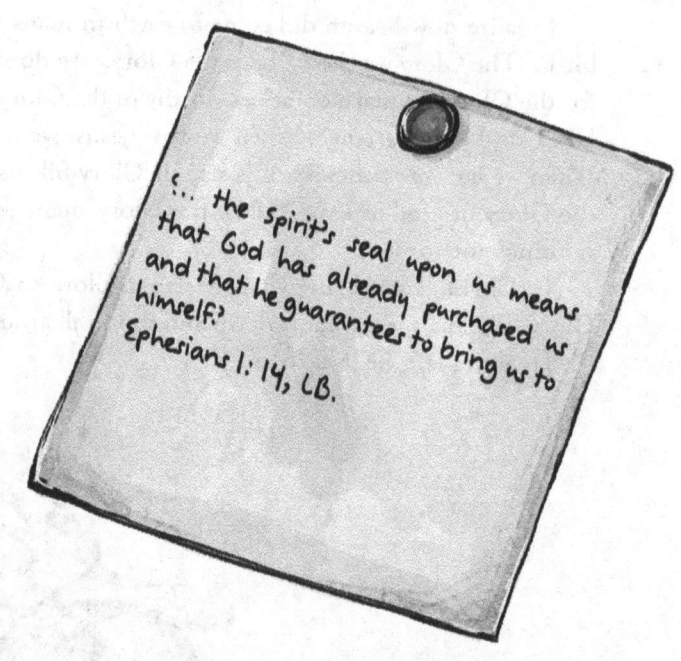

'... the Spirit's seal upon us means that God has already purchased us and that he guarantees to bring us to himself.'
Ephesians 1: 14, LB.

Letters to Anne

My dearest friend *Anne*

I am glad you accepted me as your friend.

It's a friendship I have valued greatly.

Our friendship reminds me of God, who has received us as we are.

Something to think about, scripture reading:

Ephesians 1: 6 – 8 LB '... *all praise to God for his wonderful kindness to us and his favour that he poured out upon us...*'

Accepted. My great-grandson is turning two years old, and my granddaughter, his Mum, is planning a party. His Mum has sent me an invitation to attend. I have accepted it. I look forward to the party; I'm glad I'm highly favoured enough to be invited to the party.

Remember, the announcement of Jesus birth?

The angel appeared to Mary and said, '*Congratulations, favoured lady! The Lord is with you!*' (LB) Mary was favoured by God above all other women.

God chose us before the world began; we are now beloved. The Greek translation of being '*accepted in the beloved*' means we are '*highly favoured*'.

God has poured out his approval upon us and invited us to be close to him. God approved of us because Jesus gave himself to ensure that we became acceptable and unique. God so loves us he can't love us anymore nor any less. God so loves us he gave Jesus.

For all this to become ours, we accept Jesus into our inner being. We no longer live for self but live for God. Can we accept Jesus the cherished Son and receive the Father's invitation to be his highly favoured children of God? Can we recognise we are the apple of God's eye?

God has invited us to live in his throne room with him.

We cannot go any higher nor any lower.

GWENNETH LEANE

Thought for the Day:
'Now to him who can do immeasurably more than all we ask or imagine, according to his power that is at work within us.'
Ephesians 3: 20 LB

Prayer:
Thank you, Father, for an immeasurable love, that goes beyond all we can imagine.

Notes:

Letters to Anne

Dear Anne

I appreciate your friendship.

I know I have stretched your love for me sometimes, but you have stayed my friend regardless. The word I have for our meditation today is *'immeasurable'*.

Scripture Reading:

Ephesians 3: 16 – 20. LB. V 16 *'...that out of his glorious, unlimited resources he will give you...'*

John 10: 10 LB *'The thief's purpose is to steal, kill and destroy. My purpose is to give life in all its fullness.'*

Immeasurable. When I was dressmaking, my clients came in all sizes and shapes; large and small. The tape measure didn't stretch but there were some figures that the tape was hardly big enough. Some significant forms were almost immeasurable.

The clients expected to look like a size 10 when in fact they were a size 24.

God is immeasurable himself.

All that he has created is immeasurable. Look at the galaxies – we are told they just go on forever. Stargazers said there was about 11,000 now there are countless galaxies. The distance between east and west is immeasurable. How far the east is from the west is the distance God has cast our sin from himself, which is limitless. So, our sin, past, present and future, has been placed an immeasurable distance from God. How did this happen? The Bible says *'For God took the sinless Christ and poured into him our sins. Then in exchange, he poured God's goodness into us.'* 2 Corinthians 5: 21.

Christ absorbed all our sin, he was forsaken by God while he carried that sin into the grave and when he arose from the grave, our sins were left there, cast as far as the east is from the west.

Don't let the devil tell you otherwise and steal the limitless joy of a righteous life in Christ.

'God can make it up to you by giving you everything you need and more, so there will not only be enough for your own needs but plenty left to give joyfully to others.' 2 Corinthians 9: 8 LB

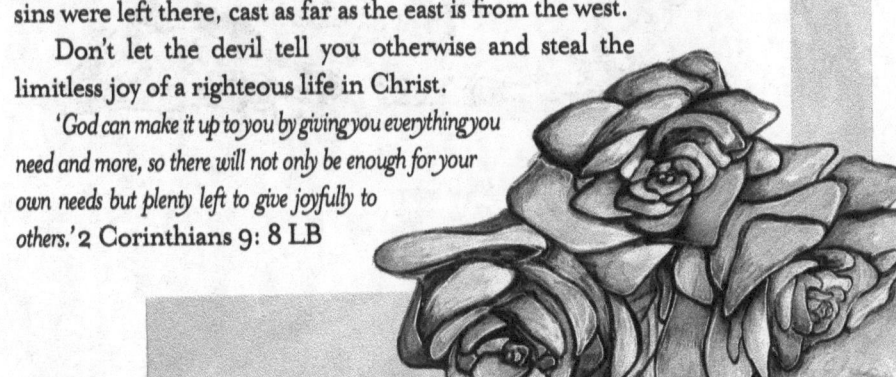

GWENNETH LEANE

Thought for the Day:
'...just think how much more surely the blood of Christ will transform our lives and hearts.'
Hebrew 9: 19 LB

Prayer:
Thank you, Father, for sending Jesus.
Thank you that Jesus came and indwelt us.
Thank you that he makes us new people.

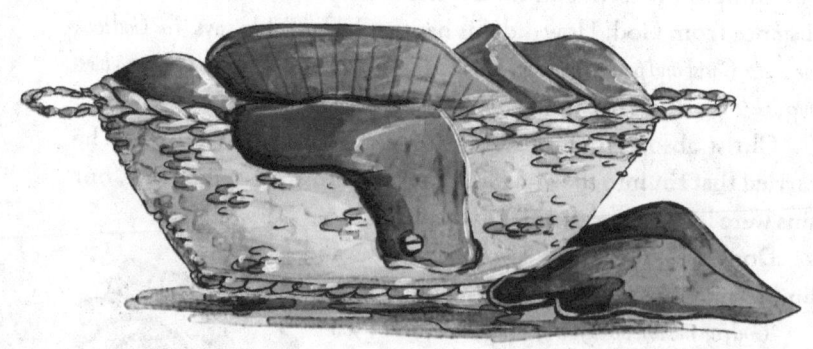

Letters to Anne

My dear Anne

Remember when we had a mud fight at the Sunday School picnic?
Remember how long it took to get the mud washed out of our hair and clothes?
Here is our scripture for today;
Colossians 2: 13 – 15.LB *'Then he gave you a share in the very life of Christ.'*
2 Corinthians 5: 21 LB *'For God took the sinless Christ and poured into him our sins. Then, in exchange, he poured God's goodness into us!'*

Washing. As a bride, I washed the clothes in a hand pump washing machine. I never called it a washing machine; it required too much effort to operate it.

I would heat water in the copper and bucket the water into the *'machine'* add soap powder, screw the large suction pump to the handle and pump up and down. The clothes were supposed to come clean. It was hard hot work still it was better than using a scrubbing board.

I remember my inadequacies, unworthiness and inability to make myself cleaner. Thinking about reinventing ourselves, we have to find a way to remove the mental dirt, the psychological baggage we accumulate throughout our life. Even our best efforts, like my washing machine action, are not perfect. We are still the same old same old, imperfect person.

God has seen our struggles, our tears, our brokenness, hopelessness and sent Jesus to us. Indeed, God laid all our imperfection on Christ on the cross. Christ bore them, he took them to the grave with him and left them there. When he arose he left our unworthiness in the grave and rose clothing us in his goodness.

When we accept Jesus, God pours into us the goodness of Jesus.

God forgets our psychological baggage; he doesn't remember it any more.

We are new people.

Our struggles are over; we just have to be.

It is not our job anymore to be better people. Jesus has made us righteous by indwelling us with himself.

GWENNETH LEANE

Thought for the Day:

I am glad that you go before me and behind me. That your hand of blessing is on my head.

Prayer:

Father, I bow in thanksgiving that you care for me, that I matter to you. Thank you that you number even the hairs on my head.

Letters to Anne

Dear *Anne*

I have some good news for you.

You matter to God, so cast your depression aside and thank him.

We'll start today with a scripture reading:
Psalm 139: 1–18. LB

This verse is fantastic: *'And he knows the number of hairs on your head! Never fear, you are far more valuable to him than a whole flock of sparrows.'* Luke 12: 7. LB

You matter. In day to day life, we often ask, do we matter?

Do we contribute to the world?

Our nation?

Are we just a face in the crowd?

To our government we are only a number, go into the shopping mall, and we take a number and stand in a queue. We have no name and wait in line until our number for our number to appear on a screen. The social engineers would have us dehumanized. No identity. No self-esteem. We are under their control.

The devil wants us to feel we are nothing because he knows he can defeat you when you believe you are worthless.

God, on the other hand, knew you before you were a twinkle in your parents' eye, he had your life planned before the womb.

You matter to God!

God calls you by name; you don't have to queue up; God personally loves you. He wants to meet your needs personally. He wants to make your life beautiful. God knows what you face because Jesus, in all points, suffered as we do.

We matter to God!

So according to scripture, God says he will always give us all we need from day to day if we make the kingdom of God our primary goal.

GWENNETH LEANE

Thought for the Day:
Jesus wants our absolute, unrestrained adoration for himself.

Prayer:
Thank you, Father, for showing us, Jesus.
Thank you, Father, for loving us so unrestrainedly.

Letters to Anne

Dear Anne

Several days ago I was reading a quote by Oswald Chambers, *'My utmost for His highest'*. These words were an inspiration to me when Oswald first penned them. At one time he was the flavour of the month as a writer. Over the years, I had forgotten the quote, but the Lord hadn't, he kept me on track growing in grace year upon year since.

Scripture Reading:

Philippians 3: 7 – 9. LB. *'I have put aside all else, counting it worth less than nothing, so that I can have Christ.'*

Verse: *'So, whatever it takes, I will be one who lives in the fresh newness of life of those who are alive from the dead.'* Philippians 3: 11, LB.

Utmost. Meditating on the word, *'utmost'* brought to mind a photo I love of my son standing alone on a high boulder on top of a mountain. Philip had conquered the peak and reached the utmost tip. There was nowhere else to go. His energy spent.

Meditating on the meaning of Oswald Chambers quote, *'my utmost for his highest'* I came to see that God requires all I am and have until there is nothing left.

He expects my utmost.

Giving our utmost brings us to a place of maturity. A relationship of trust, oneness and intimacy grow where we hang out with God, he enjoying us, and we enjoying him as we do our spouses, our children, our parents.

It is easy to give our utmost to solely hang-out with God when we see his utmost for us.

The realization of what God has provided for us eliminates the tendency to become ritualistic or going through the motions.

GWENNETH LEANE

Thought for the Day:
Keep God's truth in your head and his love in your heart.' - Zingers

Prayer:
Dear Father, thank you that Jesus is the highest prize for which we seek. We open our hearts to him to come and dwell within.

Notes:

Letters to Anne

Dear Anne

Just to let you know we are spending Easter holidays on the opal field and digging for opal. Our Aboriginal friends have infected us with opal fever. We've pegged some claims and are going to try our hand at opal mining. See you soon.

I thought this Scripture Reading was appropriate:
1 Corinthians 3: 11 – 15, LB. *'And no one can ever lay any other real foundation than the one we already have — Jesus Christ.'*

Gems. My brother Les was a fossicker of gemstones.

My husband, Bruce and I together with Les and his wife, Shirley, went on a holiday into the Hart's Range, Central Australia. Les and Shirley were intent on finding zircon and garnets. We found the Zircon field and collected what we needed. The garnets were harder to find. Eventually, Les and Shirley, after consulting the mud map decided we had arrived.

I said to Les, *'Where are the garnets?'*

'They are all around your feet. Your walking on them.'

Sure enough, the ridge of dirt thrown up by a grader along the edge of the road was full of garnets.

I have a beautiful faceted red stone of several carats.

Proverbs' 3: 15 compares wisdom as far more valuable than precious jewels. Proverbs declares that a wise man is now happier than an immediately rich person.

But the Father goes even further and says that Jesus is more valuable than precious stones. In comparison, Jesus is far more precious than gold or precious stones. He is likened to a very valuable pearl. When we see him, we sacrifice everything to be able to win him. Ephesians tell us that in Jesus, there are unlimited resources, an inner strengthening of the Holy Spirit.

When we have Jesus, we have everything.

GWENNETH LEANE

Thought for the Day:

Once you have feasted on the goodness of God, nothing else will satisfy.

Prayer:

Thank you, Father, for the clothes of righteousness you have provided for us. Thank you for Jesus that he bought our clothes with his blood.

Letters to Anne

Dear *Anne*

I was excited to hear of your coming visit. I have two tickets to the Adelaide Show. We could go to the Show together and visit the fashion parade. That would be fun.

I thought I'd have a look in the Bible to see what it said about clothes.

Sure enough, it says quite a bit.

The scripture reading is Luke 12: 22 – 32 LB. *'For life consists of far more than food or clothes.'*

Verse: *'Let me tell you how happy God has made me! For he has clothed me with garments of salvation and draped me with the robe of righteousness.'* Isaiah 61: 10, LB.

Clothes. It is incredible how we desire to dress prettily and fashionable.

Some of us like to be covered head to toe; others discard their attire until they are wearing only the stitching. Some people think it a crime to wear the same outfit twice while others don't give a care.

God spoke about our dress code; he pointed out how he clothed the flowers and the lilies in colour and beauty. If he could do this for the vegetation, what could he do for us if we trusted him?

There isn't any need to worry ourselves, just cast our cares on God, he has our physical needs in hand. God is more concerned about the state of our heart and our mental state. In our natural state, he can't enjoy an intimate relationship with us; he needs to clothe us. God, in His immeasurable love, sent Jesus to the cross, taking our failure to keep the standard he requires with him. In return, Jesus gave us his righteousness so that we could enjoy the Presence of God, and God could enjoy our company.

God gave us a gown, a robe, a suit if you like, of righteousness so that when he looked at us, he saw we wore the clothes Jesus gave us and he smiled on us. He knew Jesus indwelt us, and we lived in Jesus. Jesus and we were an entity. We were acceptable.

The only problem for us to wear the robe of righteousness we need to accept Jesus as Saviour, as the rescuer, as redeemer, as a lover.

Can we take the covering of God made possible by Jesus death? Or do we insist on trying to please God by striving to clothe ourselves with our goodness? God calls our robe of righteousness a filthy rage. He hates it. He insists we wear the suit given us by Jesus.

So, have we accepted Jesus?

GWENNETH LEANE

Thought for the Day:

Faith for any breakthrough or miracle in your life springs forth when you see Jesus and his immeasurable, mind-boggling grace.

Prayer:

Father, we thank you for the revelation of Jesus and grace we already have, but we reach toward you for even more exceptional and more precise insights of Jesus and forgiveness.

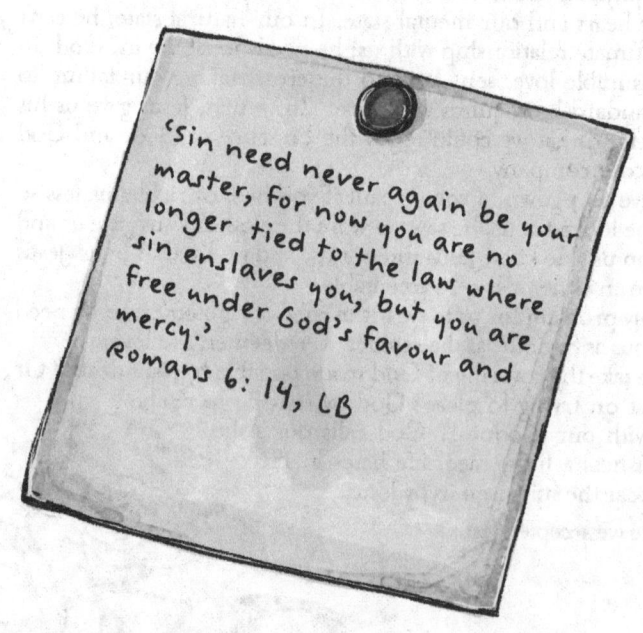

'sin need never again be your master, for now you are no longer tied to the law where sin enslaves you, but you are free under God's favour and mercy.'
Romans 6: 14, LB

Letters to Anne

Dear Anne

I have a confession to make. I ran foul of the police the other day by running a red light. I have never gone through a red light before.

An appropriate scripture: *'I ask you again, does God give you the power of the Holy Spirit and work miracles among you as a result of trying to obey the Jewish laws? No, of course not. It is when you believe in Christ and fully trusts him.'* Galatians 3: 5

Law. The Pharisees were the lawmakers, the law keepers and the lawbreakers. Their goal in life was the law and to make the law so they could keep it. They modified God's law until they were able to keep it and then imposed it on the hapless populace.

I doubt they won any popularity contests, and if they smiled, their face would crack. The word fun was not in their dictionary. To the Pharisees, the populace would not have been worth saving.

Jesus, the Son of God, sought out the woman at the well. He drank the water from her jug, and he spared her. Jesus singled out Zacchaeus, a money-grubbing crook and saved him. Jesus opened the eyes of blind Bartimaeus and removed all of his parents' guilt of sin because their son was blind.

Jesus, the sinless Son of God, was not afraid of contamination. He rubbed shoulders with the ordinary people. Jesus was the flavour of the month.

We can see two extremes. Jesus the sinless Son unafraid of being contaminated by sin and the sinful Pharisees separating themselves from the rank and file afraid of contamination. Compare Jesus to the Pharisees, and we are looking at law and grace.

Jesus, the man of grace, won the day.

He drew people to himself and healed them, freed them, made them worthy people. The Pharisees thought they had won when they crucified Jesus. They continued as lawmen, graceless, death-dealing.

Jesus, the grace man, rose from the dead.

When He arose, He raised many people with him.

Today, Jesus frees us from oppression and depression. He heals all our diseases and forgives us all our sins. Jesus is alive and well, and so are we. The lawmen never saved, healed or blessed a soul, but the grace man restores everyone who believes in him.

GWENNETH LEANE

Thought for the Day:

'Good things happen to those who know God loves them.' Joseph Prince

Prayer:

Father, thank you for loving me.
Thank you for Jesus.
Open my eyes to the truth you can do exceedingly abundantly more than we ask or think.

Notes:

Letters to Anne

Dear Anne

It's time to sit down and write you a line after several weeks of silence.

Psalm 91 is a beautiful passage of scripture. I want to share it with you.

Scripture: *'We live within the shadow of the Almighty…he alone is my refuge, my place of safety;'* Psalm 91: 1–6.

Good things. *'Good things happen to those who know God loves them.'* Joseph Prince.

The popular cliché is, *'Bad things happen to good people.'*

Bad things do happen to good people reinforcing the idea that we can expect bad things to happen. The more we believe bad things will happen, the more they do.

We know God loves us, the Word says, *'For God so loved the world that he gave his only Son…'* That is wonderful.

Next, we are told, *'God is able to do exceedingly abundant beyond all we ask or think.'* Eph 3: 20-21. That is even more wonderful. But has anything changed in our lives? Are we still struggling with circumstances and life?

Psalm 91: 1-6 pops out at us, *'He rescues us from every trap…protects us from the fatal plague…his promises are your armour… no need to fear the dangers of the day or the plagues of the night. Though a thousand fall at my side and ten thousand around me, the evil will not touch me…'* When we read this passage, our reaction is that those words are written for King David at that time; not for today. We dismiss the writings as not spoken by God and continue the struggle of life as best we can.

God loves us so much Jesus died for us, the promise is exceedingly abundant more than we ask or think. God wants our soul to prosper and be in health, he's our shield and protector. What stops us from taking God at his Word? It is our mindset? We have been taught what we can believe or can't believe but never to take God at his Word.

We need a new mindset, one that knows God truly loves us.

An understanding that God is never mad at us never listens to the tittle-tattle of others. Are we genuinely confident we are the apple of God's eye, his righteous children because of Jesus death? A new mindset will bring about confidence in the Word.

So, make sure you know God loves you.

GWENNETH LEANE

Thought for the Day:

'God wants you blessed even more than you want to be blessed.' Andrew Wommack

Prayer:

'I pray that Christ will be more and more at home in your hearts.'
Eph 3: 17 LB

'See what great love the Father has lavished on us, that we should be called the children of God! And that is what we are!'
1 John 3: 1.

Letters to Anne

Dear Anne

I just had to share with you this scripture;

Ephesians 3: 16 – 19, LB. *'Out of his glorious, unlimited resources he will give mighty inner strengthening, Christ will be more at home... living within you.'*

May your roots go down deep into God's marvellous love.

Lavish. Joseph Prince writes about God's love as being *'extravagant'*. God has spent his love on us indiscriminately. He hasn't practised any restraint in blessing us. The Father didn't consider it a waste to pour out his love on us. He dared to take the risk of his love being rejected and so spent it lavishly on us. We have not earned or merited in any way, his gifts of salvation and righteousness. All this is his real character.

God pours his love recklessly on the unworthy, the rich and poor, without fear or favour.. He does not hold anything back; his heart is on his sleeve as he sees his beloved Son nailed to the cross for our sake.

As I meditate on the excessiveness of God's love, I am speechless, stunned. The length God has gone to pour out his miracles of healing, provision, prosperity on us through-out our life is more than I can imagine. God's blessing has been on me from the day I was born. *'Who has blessed us with every blessing in heaven because we belong to Christ.'* LB

I am continually refreshed in God's love, his passion revolutionizes my life. I have seen how rich I am; I've learnt the depths that God is prepared to go to save me. I can only give him the glory, the praise, my total self.

Jesus life blood ebbed away so I could live in the place of extravagant blessing and his outrageous love. I must not waste this love by rejecting his beloved Son.

GWENNETH LEANE

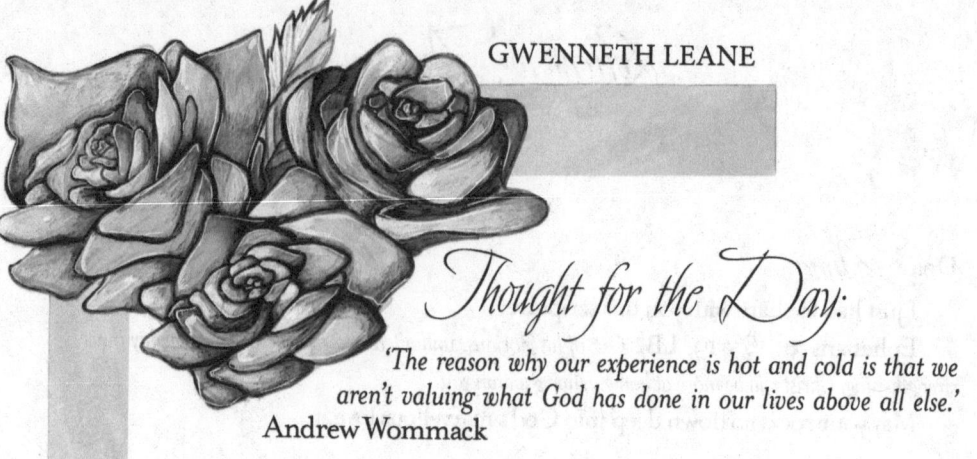

Thought for the Day:
'The reason why our experience is hot and cold is that we aren't valuing what God has done in our lives above all else.'
Andrew Wommack

Prayer:
Today I glorify you and esteem you before all else because Jesus took my beating so I could have the blessing. Thank you, Lord.

I've chosen this scripture to pin up today, Philippians 3:12, LB: 'I don't mean to say I am perfect. I haven't learned all I should even yet, but I keep working toward that day when I will finally be all that Christ saved me for and wants me to be.

Letters to Anne

Dear Anne

Dear Anne, I am sorry not to have written sooner, but life got in the way. Unfortunately, life got in the way that even God was pushed aside for a moment. I experienced firsthand his glorious grace towards me. I am more dedicated than ever as the scripture says; Philippians 3: 7 – 10 LB. *'Yes, everything is worthless when compared with the priceless gain of knowing Christ Jesus, my Lord.'*

Value. How did I lose my peace and my joy? How did I miss the presence of God? Why did I lose the blessing? And the light of revelation blackout? Who changed? What happened? Did God change his mind about me? Is he mad at me?

Life got in my way, and I didn't pursue God single-mindedly, I didn't put Christ first. I didn't value his presence, his peace and joy, his blessing, himself. I appreciated things, activities, and people more than I valued Christ. That is why the light of revelation went out. The joy of blessing died. I thought what I was doing was legitimate; it helped people; therefore, it must be right. When God loses the race in the value stakes, we are in trouble. Our peace, joy, blessing fades, stress, worry, fear fill the void.

Paul the Apostle wrote, *'What things were gain to me, those I counted loss for Christ. I count all things a loss to gain the Excellency of the knowledge of Christ. I count them dung that I might win Christ.'* Philippians 3: 7. LB

It is easy to place value on job, children, marriage, and what other people think of us and consign God to fourth or fifth position in our lives. All these things may be useful and necessary, but they should take second place and God first place. *'Seek first the kingdom of God and we won't lose any of life's necessities. God sees to it we don't lack.'*

God hasn't changed, or mad at us, departed from us.

No, we just changed our value system. Return to glorifying God, valuing him above all else as though it was dung and we'll be in heaven, in the throne room of God, enjoying his presence and doing more significant works than Christ.

GWENNETH LEANE

Thought for the Day:

How sweet the taste of God's promise is It tastes more delicious than honey.

Prayer:

Thank you, Father, for Jesus, who is the living honey and more desirable than precious stones.

I've chosen this scripture to pin up today:
Philippians 3: 12, 'LB:
'I don't mean to say I am perfect. I haven't learned all I should even yet, but I keep working toward that day when I will finally be all that Christ saved me for and wants me to be.

Letters to Anne

Dear Anne

I love honey, Anne. The Bible talks about honey and declares God's Word to be sweet and enjoyable as the nectar. Fantastic the subjects discussed in the Bible.

I've chosen for our scripture reading: '...*locusts and wild honey were his food..*'
Mark 1: 5 – 8 LB

Honey. Beekeeping has been in my family for at least two generations. My father kept bees; he needed then to pollinate the fruit trees of our orchard. Two of my brothers each kept several hundred hives. A nephew kept 300 swarms, from which he made a living.

I tried my hand at keeping two colonies in my backyard for pollination purposes. Keeping bees is a fascinating past-time. Their social structure and work ethic soon absorb one.

There is nothing as sweet as honey. God has likened his Word to be as pleasurable as this amber sweetness. Honey is mentioned 61 times in the Bible. To compare God's Word to nectar means there are riches and food for the soul found in the Word.

To meditate on God's Word is like eating honeycomb. We are soothed when sore from life's rough and tumble. We are sweetened. Honey is a sign of abundance, ease and prosperity. Jesus is not a sign; he is a real person. He came to give us abundant life beyond our imagination, comfort and well-being. God speaks of His abundant provision for the birds and flowers and declares he will provide more for us because of his great love.

We have been elevated to a luxurient position with God if we will only lay down our insistence on doing life in our way.

Believe in Jesus, accept him as saviour, live in him as a joint-heir.

Yes, Jesus can to give us abundant life.
Accept him.

GWENNETH LEANE

Thought for the Day:

'I often advocate that we look at many sides of an issue, walk in someone else's shoes, and identify and reject false choices.'
Kamala Harris.

Prayer:

Father, thank you for dressing us in your whole suit of armour, enabling us to stand in your power and strength.

Today's particular verse: Wear shoes that can speed you on as you preach the Good News of peace with God.

Letters to Anne

Dear Anne

I bought myself a pair of gorgeous shoes. I wore them shopping in the city. My pride wanted to show them off. Oh, my poor feet. They cried as I struggled to the bus stop. I soaked them in hot water and Epsom salts when I arrived home.

This scripture popped out at me: '...*a jewelled ring and shoes for his feet...*'

Shoes. Shoes are necessary to protect our feet. They are a mark of our state of mind or position in society. Shoes are also an accessory to vanity.

Women's shoes designed more for beauty rather than comfort. They are accessories of beauty, creations of art to enhance our feet. Shoes are items of ego for both men and women.

For God, shoes have meaning. Because shoes are essential to us, they are necessary to God; he can reach us through our footwear. Starting with Moses, he was commanded to take off his shoes because he was on holy ground. Discarding his shoes was a sign of obedience, humility, compliance to God and worship of his King. A way of showing God his very heart's love.

Secondly there is the story of the Prodigal Son. The son returned to his Father broken, destitute, starving. The Father saw him coming from afar and rushed around calling for a robe and a ring and shoes for his son. The Prodigal son is reminiscent of you and I. We are far from the Father, we are destitute by reason of our desire to be independent.

God has supplied us with a gown, a ring and shoes through Jesus. When Jesus died, he carried with him our poverty of spirit, our rebellion, our determination to go it alone and prove to God we could reach his standard. When we come to ourselves and come home to the Father he gives us the gown of righteousness, the ring and the shoes of peace.

God the Father embraces us and takes us into the throne room. We are restored as children of the Father and made equal with Jesus. Our shoes now are bought by the blood, sweat and tears of Jesus not by our blood, sweat and tears.

GWENNETH LEANE

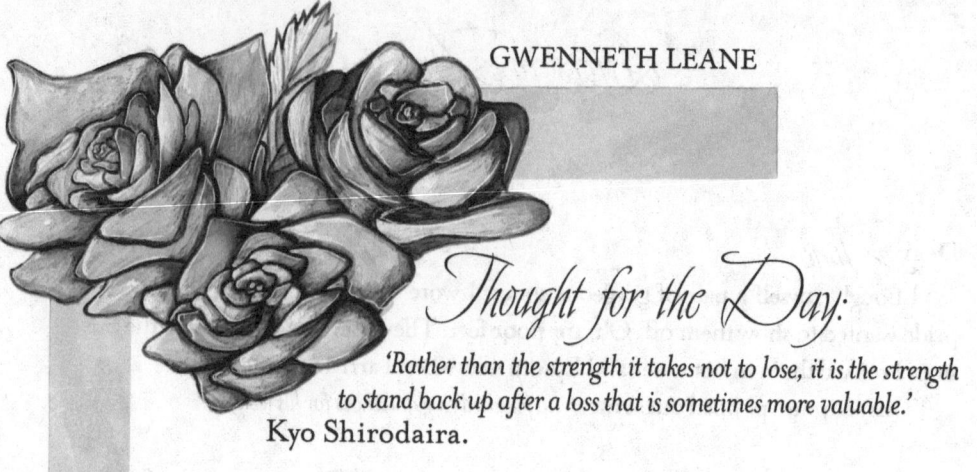

Thought for the Day:

'Rather than the strength it takes not to lose, it is the strength to stand back up after a loss that is sometimes more valuable.'
Kyo Shirodaira.

Prayer:

Thank you, Father, for Jesus righteousness that keeps us, that strengthens us, that liberates us, that causes us to stand.

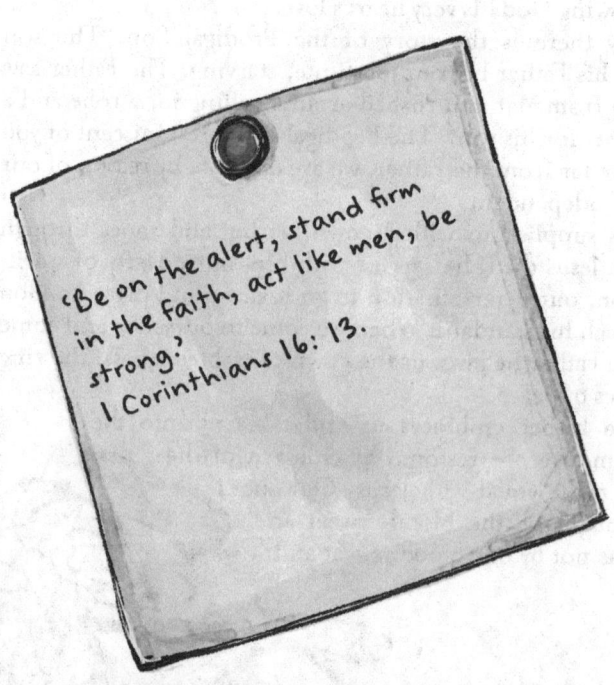

'Be on the alert, stand firm in the faith, act like men, be strong.'
I Corinthians 16: 13.

Letters to Anne

Dear Anne

I was sorry to hear about your broken leg. It will be a while before you can stand on it. Your predicament made me think about what God had to say about standing.

I thought this a suitable scripture reading:

'Christ has made us free...' Galatians 5: 1 – 4 LB

Stand. New-born babes are tiny, helpless creatures. At about four months, they become aware of their fingers and toes. Then they start practising rolling over. The look of joy at the first roll-over is beautiful. Not content at reaching that goal the struggle to stand beside furniture and anything that will support them begins. The crowning achievement comes when they walk. They are joyous. That first year has been one of persistent struggle, but they wouldn't give up.

Becoming a Christian, we start as babes.

First, we are aware that Jesus died to make us right with God, and the joy of being clean then we are aware that there is much in our life that has to change. So we set about trying to transform ourselves into what we think God wants.

Finally, we stand. We have discovered that there is nothing we can do to make God love us. We had learnt God loves us unreservedly since before the world began. The revelation bursts across our mind that Jesus died to pay for our inability to live up to God's standard. Further revelation reveals Jesus accepted our base nature as his own. The final flash of insight show Jesus gave us his character, his goodness, his inheritance.

Further truth reveals that the righteous shall stand forever. We are righteous because of Jesus. We are urged not to conform to this world system but stand firm and don't submit to the old life. Cloaking ourselves in the full armour of God so that we are able to stand against the cunning devices of the devil.

GWENNETH LEANE

Thought for the Day:

'By the Grace of God, we are highly favoured. His Grace is bigger than what our minds can ever comprehend.'
Gift Guga Mona

Prayer:

Thank you, Jesus, for taking my judgement on yourself.

Notes:

Letters to Anne

Dear Anne

I was glad to hear from you and know you are well. I have been meditating on 'grace' and have written some thoughts down and some scriptures.

Firstly the scripture reading: Romans 3: 20 – 24 LB. 'This righteousness is given through faith.'

And the Verse:

Ephesians 2: 8-9, LB *'Because of his kindness, salvation is yours through trusting Christ. And even trusting is not of yourselves; it too is a gift from God.'*

Grace. Grace is the era that I live in spiritually. My mother-in-law was called Grace. My friend's name is Grace.

God's unmerited, unearned favour, is known as Grace. Grace is God pouring out his love to us instead of his anger. We deserve his punishment; instead, he heaped the anger on Jesus. He made Jesus his scapegoat for our willful rejection. Through Jesus, we are now the beloved of God. Grace is God making us just-as-if-we'd-never-sinned.

Grace has torn down the curtain in the temple from top to bottom. No human hand touched that curtain; it was God who tore the curtain down and allowed us to enter his presence boldly through faith in Jesus.

Grace is the era when judgement, sin, and death are killed by Jesus when he died and rose again. When we are born again, we live in the presence and power of God now and forever.

When Jesus rose, he broke the power of sin.

When we are born again, Jesus empowers us to break the power of sin.

GWENNETH LEANE

Thought for the Day:

Sometimes, good things fall apart so that little thing can fall together.

Prayer:

I especially want to thank you, Lord, for Jesus and for taking a love-break and loving me before I loved you.

Letters to Anne

Dear Anne

I'm taking a break from housework to drop you a line. I'm calling it a love break because I esteem you highly as a friend and I want you to know this.

It was a great idea that we read the same scriptures together, even though we are miles apart.

Today's scripture is Romans 8: 37 – 39. *'More than conquerors…'* LB

Verse to meditate on:

Romans 5: 5. v *'Hope does not put us to shame.'*

Take a break. When I used to cut apricots for drying, it was tiring and repetitive work, we were paid so much money per tray of halved apricots. It was necessary to pace myself if I wanted to earn a decent amount of money. I worked out that I needed to cut a tray of fruit every five minutes. My cutting knife almost grew into my hand. Apricot cutters didn't take breaks.

God made the universe in six days; then he took a break. When Jesus hung on the cross and darkness covered the land, God again took a break – a hate break. He so loved the world he gave Jesus. When we are born again, we accept God's hate break. We take God's hate break where he deserted Jesus and the hate break becomes a love break and God pours out his love on us.

We need to keep taking love-breaks to tell Jesus how much we love him in return for him loving us enough to die for us.

Have you taken a love break yet?

Sit down in a quiet place and spend a few minutes meditating on the scriptures we read each day and thank him for his life in you.

GWENNETH LEANE

Thought for the Day:

'Feeling sorry for yourself and your present condition, is not only a waste of energy but the worst habit you could ever have.' Dale Carnegie

Prayer:

Thank you, Father, for Jesus, the Great Re-programmer, the Changer of habits and poor attitudes.

The verse to remember is: Romans 12: 2, 'Don't copy the behaviours and customs of this world but be a new and different person with a fresh newness.'

Letters to Anne

Dear *Anne*

I haven't changed my mind about coming to see you. It's been such a long time since we were able to have a chin-wag. I'm so looking forward to seeing you.

The scripture I've chosen for us to read and meditate on in our separate homes is Matthew 4:

19 – 23 LB. *'Jesus called out, 'Come with me.'*

Re-programmed. On average, according to jamesclear.com, it takes about 66 days to change a habit and replace it with another. It is OK to change a pattern but it has to be replaced with a new and better practice, otherwise what is the use.

We can re-invent ourselves, which gives us a great deal of satisfaction, but unfortunately, it still cuts no ice with God. If we are thinking of pleasing God and getting right with him, we need a different mindset.

To be reprogramed or re-invented, we need to take on Jesus. He clothes us with his perfections, fills us with himself. For us to be this new person, we need to be born again. We need to accept Jesus and be filled with him. When he lives in us and we in him God is pleased, he gladly accepts us as his beloved children and brings us into his presence, his throne room.

Such re-invention doesn't require 66 days; It only takes as long as we can say; *'Jesus, I accept you as my rescuer. I give my life to you. I want you to live in me and I in you.'*

Once we decide to be a child of God, no more effort is required of us to make ourselves better. Christ has done it all for us on the cross. We can say in all truth that we died with Christ: and that I no longer live, but Christ lives in me.

GWENNETH LEANE

Thought for the Day:
'Faith activates God — fear activates the enemy.'
Joel Osteen

Prayer:
Thank you, Father, that you are. That you are the Great, I AM. Thank you for showing yourself to us through Jesus.

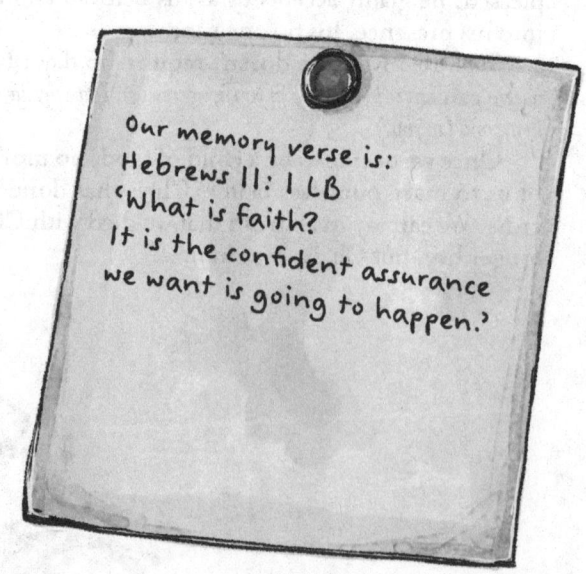

Our memory verse is:
Hebrews 11: 1 LB
'What is faith?
It is the confident assurance we want is going to happen.'

Letters to Anne

My Dear Anne

It was a pleasure to see you again.

It is beautiful the way friendships last, regardless of time and distance.

The scripture reading I chose for today is found in Hebrews 11: 6 – 12 LB

Faith. I have faith that the marmalade jam I have prepared and have on the stove cooking and which I am stirring is going to become marmalade. I have followed the recipe to the last comma; the colour is light, the bubbles are rising and breaking with a gluggy plop. My faith is in my preparation, the length of time spent cooking, the amount of sugar content and pectin. All these elements I have faith in and should reward me with excellent tasting marmalade.

God loves faith. He wants us to respond to him in faith and enjoy his presence. To enjoy the Lord, we must first believe that he is a living person. If we cannot find him and accept him, we will never see him, know him, or enjoy him.

If we commit ourselves to him and take a risk by committing to a person we can't see, what will the outcome be? The answer is yes! God will reward our faith, we'll reward his faith in us, we'll see him, we'll know him, we'll enjoy him.

God has promised us a life of abundance, joy, peace, everlasting life, protection and provision. It all rests on us taking a risk and putting our faith in him.

God will be happy; we will be satisfied.

The world will be a better place and heaven more populous.

GWENNETH LEANE

Thought for the Day:

I feel the healing hands of God, touching my heart and kiss my soul.' Harley King.

Prayer:

You touch, Lord, is life to me.
Thank you for Jesus whose touch carry's healing.

A verse to remember:
Luke 6: 19 LB,
'Everyone was trying to touch him, for when they did healing power went out from him, and into them and they were cured.'

Letters to Anne

Dear Anne

Just a quick note to touch base with you.

I was thinking about 'touching base', and the story of the woman who wanted to touch Jesus clothes because she thought she might be healed. Strange how the brain connects words and events.

A good scripture reading for today would be Mark 6 24 – 34 LB. *'If I can just touch his clothes...'*

Touch. In caring for older people, carers are encouraged to touch them on the shoulder, the hand, the arm. The caress, whether we are old or young, is so vital in making a person feel wanted, needed, loved, and esteemed, of worth. Older people become isolated for many reasons and are not touched.

A woman after her husband had passed away, confided that the most significant thing she missed was the touch of her husband.

Jesus touched many people and healed them. Nothing has changed, Jesus still affects people, and they are repaired, restored, in spirit and body. Jesus desires contact with us more than we want his touch. Jesus touch still heals today.

When God touches us, we recognise how empty we are and how deeply we yearn for his touch. The human touch is fleeting, but the touch of God never fades.

Jesus death was a means to open the door for God to win us, to touch us, heal us, give us n abundance of life. There is so much fulness, completeness in the touch of God. When we reach out and touch God's heart, we are overwhelmed by a love so unfathomable we can only surrender ourselves and live for his touch.

GWENNETH LEANE

Thought for the Day:
'Experience is the name we give our mistakes.'
Oscar Wilde.

Prayer:
Thank you, Father, for Jesus, whose name saves us.

Notes:

Letters to Anne

Dear Anne

The question of what's in a name arose the other day.

A search revealed that Anne meant popularity.

The name Anne also has origins in Hebrew, French and English. It is interesting that in the Bible, surnames often had prophetic meaning. I thought I would see what the scriptures say about names:

Genesis 17: 15 – 21. '... –her name is no longer 'Sarai' but 'Sarah' ('Princess').

The memory verse indicates a name change:

Ruth 1: 20. LB *'Don't call me Naomi. Call me Mara'* (Naomi means "pleasant"; Mara means bitter).'

Names. What's in a name? Biblically speaking, there is plenty in the meaning of a name. Out of curiosity, I decided to look up the meaning of the name Gweneth. I discovered that Gweneth was a Welsh name. It means blessed. People with the name Gweneth are supposed to have a deep inner desire to use their abilities in leadership. It's called 'soul urge'.

I don't believe the meaning of my name has anything to do with my character. But I have longed to feel blessed, and fair or good-looking. I have a deep desire to use my abilities in the service of God. So perhaps I have lived up to my name.

What's in a name you ask? What's in the name of Jesus? The name of Jesus means 'deliverer', 'rescuer'. It is a Hebrew name. From the moment Jesus was conceived, his name was to be Jesus, he would save his people. From his birth, his mission was to save we humans from our bondage to sin. He was to rescue us from our separation from the Father.

Jesus bore many names referring to his royalty, such as:
'Wonderful', 'Counsellor,' 'The Mighty God,' 'Prince of Peace.'
He fulfilled all these names.

There is no other name we can call upon to rescue us, to deliver us, to restore us and make us new people.

Remember the name of Jesus.

Jesus saves any and everyone who calls on his name.

GWENNETH LEANE

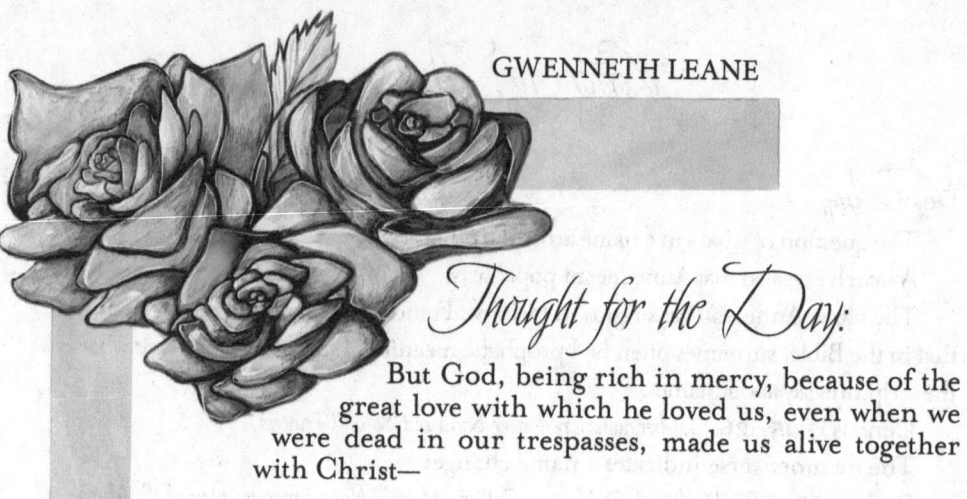

Thought for the Day:

But God, being rich in mercy, because of the great love with which he loved us, even when we were dead in our trespasses, made us alive together with Christ—

Prayer:

Dear Father, open our minds, so we realize that because you love us extravagantly, you give us new, unused mercies every day.
Thank you for your faithfulness.

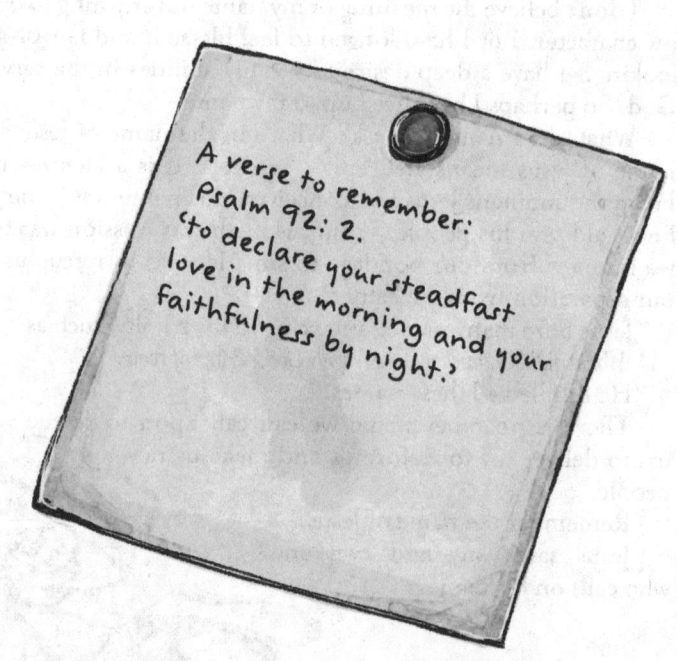

A verse to remember:
Psalm 92: 2.
'to declare your steadfast love in the morning and your faithfulness by night.'

Letters to Anne

Dear Anne

I wanted to say how much I appreciate being your friend for so many years. We don't always meet, but our friendship is still fresh and new.

Catching up on our scripture reading in Lamentations 3: 21-26.
'Every morning tells him, "Thank you for your kindness," and every evening rejoice in all His faithfulness.'

New! New often means it has never been worn before or used by anyone before. It is as pristine as the creator can make it. It means that something is different such as different clothes, different food.

The Bible speaks of mercies that are new every day. Does that mean these mercies are fresh and new, especially for that day only? That each day there is new mercy given by God?

This morning's new mercies are for today; tomorrow will see a different set of mercies or blessings.

Yesterday's mercies are not for today.

They are yesterday's blessing and are gone.

God has new mercies for us tomorrow.

God gave the children of Israel fresh manna every day. If they tried to collect extra and keep it, it went perished. The same applies to the mercies of God.

We remember yesterday's mercies for our encouragement. Yesterday's generosities become too familiar and we ignore them, cease to be grateful. We cannot keep them for today.

God is steadfast; he doesn't forget to create new mercies for us every day. Just as he was constant and faithful to the Israelites in the wilderness, so is he to us. We receive new mercies every day; we just need to collect them and not continually live on yesterday's indulgences.

Great is God's faithfulness – the faithfulness of God is mind-blowing, crazy, no logic to why God, each day, pours out new mercies not used before by anyone.

GWENNETH LEANE

Thought for the Day:

'Because he bends down and listens, I will pray as long as I breathe.'
Psalm 116: 2.

Prayer:

I worship you and offer you praise and thanksgiving for saving me, protecting me, providing for me daily.

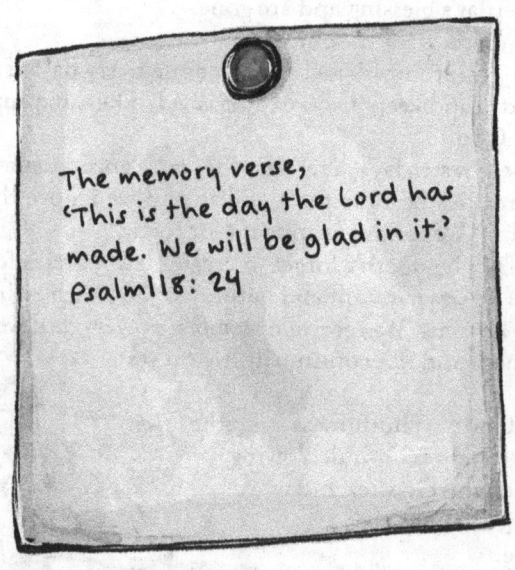

The memory verse,
'This is the day the Lord has made. We will be glad in it.'
Psalm 118: 24

Letters to Anne

Dearest Anne

Life is very precarious and no matter whether our job is secure, our house is paid for, and we have done all we can to stay safe and secure, fear of the unknown is always present. Today I found a comforting scripture reading:

Psalm 121: 1 – 8.

'He protects you day and night...'

Daily. For our health and well-being, we eat every day. Most of us indulge in three meals plus snacks. It sometimes feels one has one meal a day with meals, morning and afternoon teas and snacks in between.

It's essential to stay hydrated and maintain our energy level. So, to add to the daily program, drink plenty of fluids. Adding to the daily routine of eating is the need to exercise. All this to stay healthy.

It is crucial to stay healthy; it leads to a long life, a good life, a productive life. All of this must happen daily.

The most critical part requires a daily routine of care. Our walk with God is daily. God loves us and wants to be involved with us each day. The Lord makes every day, he never sleeps or slumbers, but is alert to our every need or desire.

Every day is with the Lord because he has chosen to dwell within us. *'It is no longer I that is alive, but Christ who lives within me. Therefore, God is with us daily, he never leaves.'*

Psalm 116 speaks about how we can relax because the Lord is kind; he is righteous, so merciful daily. Not once a week, or month but daily, he pours out blessings on us.

GWENNETH LEANE

Thought for the Day:

"Three may keep a secret if two of you are dead."
Benjamin Franklin.

Prayer:

Thank you for revealing Jesus as Saviour.
Thank you, Jesus is no longer a secret but exposed to the whole world as the reconciler.

'But now you belong to Christ Jesus, and though you were once far away from God, now you have been brought very near to him. Because of what Jesus has done for you with his blood.'
Ephesian 2: 13. LB.

Letters to Anne

Dearest *Anne*

Being a Christian has its ups and downs, but when we accepted Christ into our lives, the comfort of his presence and power carried us through those ups and downs easier than if we were battling through on our own.

Our scripture reading speaks of God, revealing his secret.

Ephesians 1: 9 – 12. *'God has told us his secret reason for sending Christ...'*

Secrets. *'If it is not your story to tell you don't tell it.'* Lyanla Vanzantu.

When I was little, I could never keep a secret. My siblings would say, *'Don't tell Mum.'*

Of course, I would tell mum at the first opportunity. My siblings would get into trouble, and in their hurt and anger, they would turn on me, and I would suffer at their hands.

As I grew up, I learned not to tell another's story and kept my own counsel and their secrets.

Is it a sin to keep secrets? Yes and no. It depends on what the information is. Very personal stories are best left untold, even forgotten. Some stories are public and talked over in detail. Nothing is hidden.

Today, God has given we believers the responsibility to tell the story of Jesus. Once, at the beginning of time, God kept Jesus a secret. Two thousand years ago, he revealed Jesus as the go-between himself and us. We are to accept Jesus, make him our elder brother, as it were. It is no secret anymore that Jesus is the son of God and the one who bridged the gap between God and us. When we believe and accept Jesus as the revealed and beloved son of God, we become the precious children. There are no secrets anymore between God and us.

Today, we have the responsibility to tell the world about Jesus.

How we have been made new people when we believe and accept Jesus.

GWENNETH LEANE

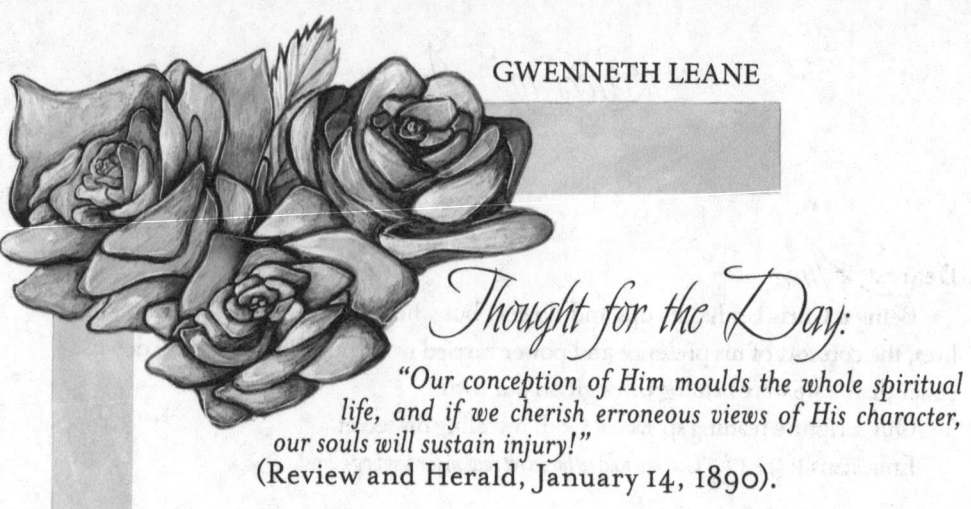

Thought for the Day:

"Our conception of Him moulds the whole spiritual life, and if we cherish erroneous views of His character, our souls will sustain injury!"
(Review and Herald, January 14, 1890).

Prayer:

Thank you, Father, for Jesus. We rejoice we can be with you forever in Jesus, that nothing can separate us.'

Letters to Anne

Dear Anne

We will be attending the Health Conference next week. I am hoping to catch up with you then. It will be wonderful to spend the lunch hour together.

I love this scripture reading:

Isaiah 42: 5-8, *'I the Lord have called you to demonstrate my righteousness...'* LB

I feel amazed by God having secrets? This verse says so:

Romans 16: 25 – 27: *'This is God's plan of salvation for you Gentiles, kept secret from the beginning...'* LB

Secrets. A blabber-mouth, that was me as a child. I had to tell Mum everything. My older siblings hated me.

As I grew up, I learned to keep my counsel and not speak. In the end, I learned to hold my tongue, to remain silent. I went from one extreme to the other, becoming a closed book. I was still unpopular, but with a different group of people. People who wanted to know all about the confidences of others. In other words, they were gossipers and needed me to reveal all I knew about people.

Even God had secrets which he kept until the right time, and then he poured out his heart to humanity. He held nothing back.

God had a secret plan; a plan made far back in eternity before ever the world was created. He would send Jesus to live among us, and Jesus would be his exact likeness. We would then accept God as our Father and be his children and intimately enjoy his company. *'God has told us his secret reason for sending Christ, a plan he decided on in mercy long ago; and this was his purpose: that when the time is ripe, he will gather us all together from wherever we are – in heaven or earth – to be with him in Christ forever.'* Ephesians 1: 9.LB.

Jesus was the secret God kept hidden for aeons; then he revealed him, first as a babe, then as a preacher and healer and finally, a sacrifice. Jesus is no longer a secret but a saviour for all the world to see, know and accept.

Do you know Jesus as a Saviour? Or is he still a secret to you? Hidden.

GWENNETH LEANE

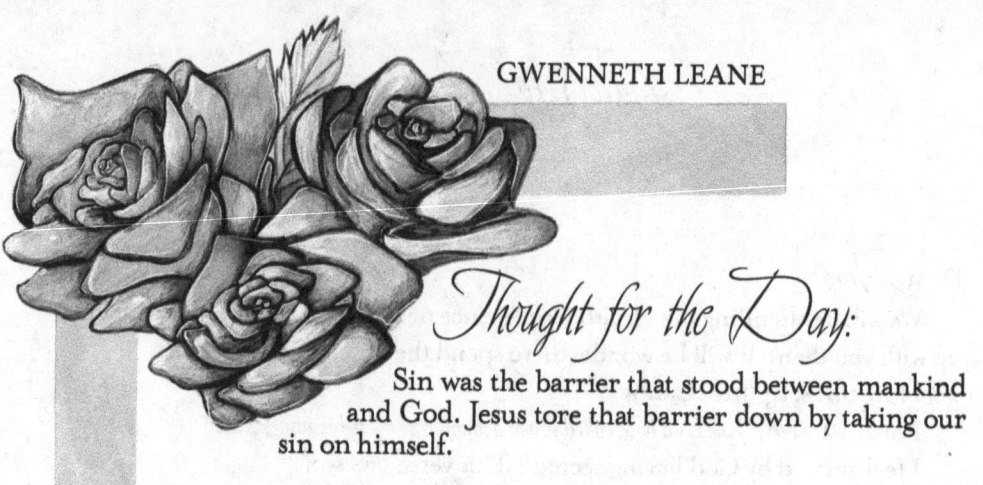

Thought for the Day:

Sin was the barrier that stood between mankind and God. Jesus tore that barrier down by taking our sin on himself.

Prayer:

Thank you, Father, for tearing down the barriers so we can enjoy your beautiful presence.

> Christ has brought you into the very presence of God, and you are standing there before him with nothing left against you...'
> Colossians 1: 22, LB.

Letters to Anne

Dear Anne

Your email was very newsy. I felt glad that all was well with you. The reading I chose for today I thought was especially relevant.

Scripture to study Colossians 1: 20-23. *'Peace with God for all by his blood...'*

Barriers is a word that conjures up in our mind different kinds of images. For instance, borders around countries, the moat around castles, rivers. High walls, fences, screens on doors and window for protection. Barriers supposedly keep someone in or something out.

There is a barrier that divides Australia. It is a simple fence that stretches across the land for from the cliffs at Nundroo, South Australia on the Great Australia Bight to Goondiwindi Queensland. The Fence runs for 5, 300 km.

Looking at the Fence, commonly known as the Dog Fence, it is so simple and ordinary one wonders what it keeps out. The Fence is vital for the economy of the country it protects. The enemy is the wild dogs or dingos that roam freely north of the Fence. Wild dogs are killers; they can decimate a flock of sheep in a night.

There is a barrier that surrounds us humans. The barrier of problems, sicknesses, mental ills, addictions. We seem unable to break free, to escape from these restrictions.

Standing above us is a rough wooden cross; it is simple, ordinary, and unpretentious. It divides the world. One either believes or rejects the man hanging there. He is the average man, also the heavenly man. He is Jesus, come to save us, mentor us. He is our elder brother.

We can reject Jesus at our peril, or we can accept him. In rejecting Jesus, we declare our independence from God and the way is dark and hard. Accept Jesus, and we become the beloved of the Father by faith in Jesus.

GWENNETH LEANE

Thought for the Day:

For where your treasure is, there will be your treasure.

Prayer:

Father, reveal to us the hidden treasures in Christ.

Letters to Anne

Dear *Anne*

it has been some time since we have met. I expect your children have grown up, married and have children of their own. God has challenged my love for Christ that it is a shallow, superficial love. Why, because of our scripture reading, Colossians 2: 1–3 LB *'In him lie all the mighty, untapped treasures of wisdom and knowledge.'*

What a powerful verse: *'Since you became alive again, so to speak, when Christ arose from the dead, now set your sights on the rich treasures and joys of heaven where he sits beside God in the place of honour and power.'* Colossians 3: 1 LB

Seek treasure. Christopher and Robert, two blonde-haired boys of six and eight years of age, sons of my best friend, were an imaginative pair.

They were rich and in possession of a treasure chest of gold and jewels beyond rich. The treasure chest was theirs because they had fought the pirates and won the treasure. They had it all.

Two pairs of blue eyes glowed with the fire of adventure as they dug a hole on a sandy beach under a palm tree on an island in the Ocean of Nowhere. They marked the spot X on a map they had made of crocodile skin.

A battle with the enemy ensued. Chris and Rob had hidden in the jungle but alas the angry pirates discovered them. The two boys fought to the last breath. They were left battered, bleeding and bruised, but the enemy were all dead to a man.

The dream faded. The treasure vanished. All that was left were pieces of broken tile, bits of timber, a plastic funnel and scraps of rubber. The tropical island faded to become a suburban backyard, filled with the paraphernalia of a family. The ordinary took over.

There is a treasure that doesn't vanish, that doesn't tarnish, that never loses its value. A wealth that lights up our life with joy, love, peace. In today's world of mental illness, homelessness and poverty, these are treasures that glow white-hot in the darkness.

Where do we find this treasure? The map is the Bible. It will tell us all we need to know about how to find the treasure. The treasure I'm talking about is Jesus, God's Son.

When we have Jesus, we have everything, untapped treasures of wisdom and knowledge.

GWENNETH LEANE

Thought for the Day:

Grace is when God gives us what we don't deserve.
Mercy is when God doesn't give us what we do deserve.

Prayer:

Thank you, Father, that Jesus ushered in the age of grace, making it possible for me to be your beloved.

Notes:

Letters to Anne

Dear Anne

It is becoming difficult this year with the Covid – 19 rampant around the world. All our traditions challenged. We have had to invent a new way of celebrating old traditions. The Bible, as usual, points out the truth about traditions.

A good scripture to read is Galatians 9: 11, *'But now you have come to know God...how is it that you turn back again...'*

For meditation, this verse: Ephesians 2; 20 LB, *'What a foundation you stand on now: the apostles and prophets; and the cornerstone of the building is Jesus Christ himself.'*

Traditions. Most family dynasties have cultures that date far back in the past. Each family discards some traditions and adds new ones that suit the times better. Traditions come and go.

I think God is the same; he set up traditions in the Old Testament. There were the Ten Commandments, then the Tabernacle worship and its sacrifices. The Prophets built Altars to commemorate significant events and in the life of the nation of Israel.

Finally, God did away with the ritual of animal sacrifice for sin. He replaced animal sacrifices with Jesus who died once for all. Thus, no more sacrifices were needed. Jesus fulfilled all the traditions of the past.

The Old Testament is just that a testament of laws, sacrifices that didn't give God the relationship with us that he so desired.

The Ten Commandments only showed God and us that we could not keep these traditions; It was not in us to sustain the standard God required for a relationship. Another culture must be created, implemented for him to reach his goal for us and for us to be able to relate to God intimately. A new tradition was born, the age of grace.

The new tradition requires us to accept Jesus and invite him into our heart and be born again. By doing this, we become new people, under a new regime. A regime that says, we are just as if we had never sinned.

GWENNETH LEANE

Thought for the Day:

'Believe in God as you believe in the sunrise. Not because you can see it, but because you can see all it touches.'
CS Lewis.

Prayer:

I praise you that Jesus shone into my life. That he leads me, sh0ows me the way of truth and that I walk in his brilliant light.

Notes:

Letters to Anne

Dear Anne

This morning I saw a beautiful sunrise. It reminded me that God had given us a new start.

I was refreshed by reading this scripture:

Isaiah 53: 2 – 6 *'Yet God laid on him the guilt and sins of every one of us.'*

The sunrise heralded a new start, so does this verse:

'Therefore, if anyone is in Christ Jesus he is a new creature, the old things passed away, behold, new things have come.'

Sunrise. When we were opal mining at Mintabie in the remote north of South Australia, we would get up at the crack of dawn. The plan was to be down the mine before the heat-blasted us.

When the sun burst over the horizon, we would be hard at work. Because as soon as the sun broke across the landscape, the flies descended, and the heat rose. By lunchtime it was so hot we had to find relief in our camp or someplace where it was cool.

Aboriginal people called the dawn pickaninny light when the sky turned white and black shadow lined the horizon. The heavens would change colour, and the black lace outlines of tree take shape. Finally, the sun, blazing in all its power broke above the horizon. The mystery of the night was only a memory until the sun dropped below the horizon in the west.

A new light has dawned within us.

That light is Jesus.

The Bible refers to him as the light of the world and as a great inner light.

When we accept him and take him into our heart and are born again, we live in the blazing sunlight of his presence. Jesus referred to himself as the way, the truth and the light. Jesus was trying to say that he gave direction on what to do. He was the truth, also he dealt in reality. The truths he spoke of set us free and the light he spoke of would lead us beside calm waters. Jesus contains all we need, and we can safely commit ourselves to him and not hold back.

GWENNETH LEANE

Thought for the Day:

When God pardons sin, he purges the record, erases the remembrance, and empowers the recipient.' Zingers.

Prayer:

Father, thank you for opening my cage and allowing me to fly free in Jesus.

Notes:

Letters to Anne

Dear Anne

You have been much in my thoughts these last weeks.

Hope all is well with you.

With the Covid 19 virus raging around the world and creating social havoc not seens since World War 2, I am wondering how you are managing.

Scripture reading:

Psalm 91 LB. *'This I declare, he alone is my refuge, my place of safety.'*

I just had to choose this verse, Psalm 91: 3 LB *'For he rescues you from every trap, and protects you from the fatal plague.'*

Caged. When my children were young, like most families, we kept a budgie in a small cage. His name was Georgie. Because he was a young bird alone, we were able to teach him to talk. 'Hello Georgie' and 'Pretty boy'. I used to talk to him a lot.

I hated seeing him in such a tiny cage where he could not fly free, and I tried to choose times when I could let him out inside to fly.

You've guessed it, one day he escaped outside.

He was gone forever.

It was a cold, wet day; he had never learnt to look after himself; he would not have survived very long. His freedom would have brought about his death. We, humans, are in a similar predicament, though we may not recognize it. Caged by our failures, depressions, addictions and lusts, we cannot escape. God saw our dilemma; he saw we were caged. I loved little Georgie, God loved us without limit and cause, his love was unconditional, and so he wanted us to be free of our cages.

Jesus opened the cage door of our sicknesses and mental problems when he died. We can escape the cage when we accept Jesus and are born again. We are new people with a new heart and a new mind.

My budgie would have died I was dead spiritually and mentally, when I believed, accepted Jesus and gave my life to him, my cage opened, and I lived. I saw the world through different eyes, God's eyes.

I could say, *'The life I now live, I live by the faith of Jesus Christ.'*

GWENNETH LEANE

Thought for the Day:

It is only with the heart that one can see rightly, what is essential is invisible to the eye.'
Antoine de Saint-Exupery.

Prayer:

Please Jesus come into my heart this day. I want to live a new life in Christ. Thank you for Jesus, who killed the virus called sin.

Letters to Anne

Dear Anne

You have been in my thoughts consistently this last week. I trust you are well. I have been thinking about many types of the virus such as depression, poor self-esteem, addictions to drug, food and what is called retail therapy. Not recognized as viruses, they can defeat us if we give way to them

I thought this scripture is appropriate:

Galatians 5: 1 – 6 LB *'So, Christ has made you free...'*

How hard we find it to believe this verse: *'You were dead in sins, and your sinful desires were not yet cut away. Then Jesus gave you a share in the very life of Christ, for he forgave all your sins.'* Colossians 2: 13. LB

Vulnerable. Vulnerable is a popular word for old age, babies, and anyone in between that is sick. Referring to people who are exposed to sickness as 'vulnerable' is suppose to make them feel better about themselves. It is political correctness for tolerance. It is labelling people into a category without saying they are stereotyped.

The virus Covid 19 is raging around the world; there is hardly a nation on the globe not touched by it. All social structures have turned upside down, leaving everyone wondering what will be.

Not since World War 2 has the world been turned upside down. After the war, a great social change took place. After the virus is over, there will again be significant social change.

There is a worse virus rampant in the world, the infection of sin. Nevermore, do we see evidence of this virus than when crises of hardship, shortages, are upon us. The best and the worst of our sin nature rises. It is in times of such challenges that we see our true selves, and often we don't like what we see.

God has stepped in; He has killed the virus of sin. It is dead. We are no longer in isolation from God but in his presence. The infection of sin perished when Jesus died on the cross. He completely removed the virus from our hearts and gave us new hearts and new minds. Jesus united us with himself as one.

To enjoy the new life, we need to accept Jesus and be born again.

To understand that as Jesus was raised from the dead killing the sin virus, God raised us, investing in us the life of Christ.

Be healed this day from the sin virus by inviting Jesus into our heart and becoming new people and enjoying the start of abundant eternal life.

GWENNETH LEANE

Authors Note:

A book of devotions was conceived in the mists of the past. It has been in Gwen's heart seemingly forever to share love breaks with the Lord each day.

The book is birthed and brought to fruition by a series of emails to a friend. The emails, originally, were written to encourage a friend experiencing dark moments. The thoughts made into a collection of daily inspirations was the next step and so Letters to Anne was born.

It could well occur that a year's collection is written over time.

Many daily devotion collections have been written and why add another collection? Step by step the Lord led Gwen to write the series of letters to a friend, thus they are more intimate than daily devotions. They are short pieces and easily read on the run. Gwen looks on them as love breaks with the Lord.

It is in Gwen's heart that the immensity of what Jesus has done and given to us is shared so that we know Jesus and learn we are the beloved of the Father. As Jesus is so are we in this world.

Letters to Anne

www.ingramcontent.com/pod-product-compliance
Lightning Source LLC
Chambersburg PA
CBHW010449010526
44118CB00019B/2520